Another Chance
III

Claire McClennan

HRB

HOLROCKS BOOKS

First Published in 2000 by HolRocks Books
PO Box 107
Paignton
Devon
TQ4 7YR

ANOTHER CHANCE III

A CIP catalogue record for this book
is available from the British Library

ISBN 0 – 9526944 – 3 - 3

Printed and Bound in Great Britain by Henry Ling Ltd. at The Dorset Press, Dorchester, Dorset

WHY ?

The baby camel looked up at his mother.

'Why,' he asked, *'have I got a huge hump on my back?'*

'The hump,' replied his mother, *'is to store water in*

as we treck across the desert sands.'

'Why have I got such large feet?'

'Your large feet prevent you sinking knee-deep

into the sand on the hot dusty trails.'

'Why have I got such long eyelashes?'

'Your eyelashes keep the stinging sand away from your eyes

when the sand storms rage.'

'Why then,' whispered the baby camel,

'am I living in a zoo?'

Anon.

CONTENTS

PAGE

*'If you love animals, they love you in return –
it's as simple as that.'*

Elizabeth Oliver, Animal Refuge, Kansai.

Little Swag, the orphaned wombat.

SWAG
EENY, MEANY, MINY & MO

THE YOUNG WILDLIFE OF TASMANIA

*Five orphaned rascals, whose rehabilitation
brought mayhem, fun and much laughter!*

'Escaping to the far north-east of Tasmania for a private weekend,' recalls Nick Mooney, who works with the Wildlife Service in Tasmania, 'my new girlfriend and I were dawdling along in her beetle, contemplating the hot January morning and discussing wants and not wants.'

'As a Wildlife Officer on tour, I was showing off. *"What could I possibly do for you, Kate?"* I asked and she remarked, *"I've always wanted to look after an orphaned wombat!"'*

With it's short tail and legs, characteristic waddle and cuddly appearance, it's closest relative being the koala, the wombat is one of the most endearing of Australia's native animals. Now a protected species in Tasmania, they can be found on heathland, coastal scrub and open forest, digging burrows with numerous connecting tunnels and entrances.

'Well,' continues Nick, 'barely had the words gotten out and I happened to glance sideways through the forest along an old track running perpendicular to the road. I'll never forget the fleeting image.'

'There, 10m. away, was a barely furred grapefruit, plodding belatedly towards us, complete with a little dust trail. Now, wombats this small are *never* on their own, *never* out in the day and if they are, they are in *alot* of trouble! I knew too, that such small animals can disappear into the undergrowth in a flash.'

'"STOP AND REVERSE!" I yelled. Kate eyed me suspiciously and by the time we reached the track I was half out of the car hurling myself into the scrub! In retrospect, I was lucky Kate did not roar off in search of less maniacal company. But, I'm a great believer in fortune favouring the bold.'

© NM

Big Trouble ahead!
Swag and Kate.

'I had caught the wombat and scooped her up before she was actually aware what was impending. She was so exhausted that all she did was curl up and push her nose into my cupped hands, rolling up her monstrous, flat feet.'

'To say I had earned countless DCP's (Domestic Credit Points) was an understatement. Kate yelped with surprise and after brief congratulations, I was temporarily forgotten in the fuss over the wombat's wellbeing.'

'After a brief search, I found the predictable – an adult female wombat, road-killed several days before.'

'We now had the little orphan. Like all her kin, this little wombat was incredibly robust and that probably saved her from critical dehydration. She was also so lucky not to have been found by a roving Tasmanian Devil or Wedge-tailed Eagle.'

'Unbelievable luck followed. We found some special marsupial milk mix under the car seat – forgotten surplus from a delivery to an animal carer – and I found my puffer camera cleaner made the perfect bottle and teat. Swag – our newly named little wombat – seemed content to rest wrapped up under Kate's jumper. So we beetled on.'

'Arriving back in Hobart, Kate's mother Ginni, (my mother outlaw to be), took one look at Swag, was so taken by her – that was it! With a glare, Ginni declared us incompetent, pointing out all the ticks we had missed and she soon was to take over.'

'Now, nothing dares die if Ginni is looking after it. Swag's re-education of the household soon began. The little wombat orphan became so addicted to Ginni's grooming that at the slightest respite, she would hurl herself on her back, preferably on someone's lap, to be scratched.'

'On the rare occasion Poppy, the family labrador, and Swag found themselves together, marsupialism reigned. Poppy quickly learned to stand, tiptoe on chair, as the wombat prowled about like a shark looking for fresh victims to sleep on. Swag knew Poppy was there somewhere, but just could not find the warm, fluffy body to snuggle up on. I will always remember Poppy leaning forward, trying to see if Swag was under the chair waiting to ambush!'

'Everyone and everything was held to ransom by our little wombat. Swag even bullied Mac, the Forester Kangaroo, whom Ginni was rearing. Nips on the tail, soon propelled the giant joey in bounds around the house creating the mayhem that wombats seem to find necessary. To everyone's relief, Swag adopted a teddy, twice her size, dragging it to and fro, occasionally collapsing on it for a snooze.'

'Like all juvenile wombats, Swag was personable, playful and eccentric. Over the next few months, she markedly decreased the house value but with the stream of native animals being rehabilitated, she seemed to hold a good grip on wombat reality. Weaning onto coarse grasses and chair legs, she went literally from strength to strength and over the next five months wrecked all our, and then others', rehabilitation facilities, to the point where she support-released herself at around 10 kg.'

'Starting at a tiny 400g. and with no future, our experience with a dusty little Swag was a *huge* success.'

'No wonder rehabilitators almost fight over orphaned wombats.'

• • • •

For Nick, yet another wonderful rehabilitation experience started late one July night, with a dark shadow hurrying across a country road. This was no ordinary shadow; it was an 8 kg. Tasmanian Devil.

The Tasmanian Devil is the world's largest surviving marsupial. It's spine-chilling screeches, dark coat and reputed bad temper led early settlers to call it 'The Devil', yet although only the size of a small dog, it can sound and look incredibly fierce. However, the famous yawn of the devil, that looks so threatening, can be misleading, as it appears more from fear and uncertainty than from aggression.

For over a century, these animals were trapped and poisoned and became very rare and seemed to be heading for extinction. But now the population is protected by law, has gradually increased and is now safe.

'This particular Tasmanian Devil,' continues Nick, 'was unlucky that night. She was hit hard by a car and killed instantly.'

'But a passing Parks and Wildlife Service Ranger saw the dark bundle on the roadside and stopped to check it, fully expecting yet another sad tale. However, in her pouch, the Ranger could see four squirming black and white tennis ball sized young. A few days later and these young, at an unmanageable size for being in their mother's pouch, would have been left in a den and would have starved with the loss of their mother. Or maybe, unencumbered by the quartet, she would have eluded the car.'

'Whatever, Ms. Ranger soon had her hands full with a squirming, squealing hat full and too much else to do!'

'Taking them home, the three young males and one female, all with individual markings giving them convenient identification, were quickly weighed coming in at 170g. and checked for injuries. Straight away, their need for psychological security, through touching, was obvious; they burrowed and snuggled into armpits and each other for warmth. They had never been left alone and they quickly whined in protest if left untouched.'

'Two hours later, they were tentatively sucking at a milk mix and tucked up into a woollen hat complete with hot water bottle!'

'Feeds had to be every four hours and Ms. Ranger found she could no longer cope.'

Nick was widely known for his fetish for Tasmanian Devils. He rescues young devils from under houses where they are incredibly noisy and people just can't tolerate them. Rearing them in a group is essential, as these animals have very complex social behaviours. There was nothing else for it. The four rascals would have to be handed over to Nick and Kate!

'They arrived with us in good condition, already with different temperaments,' remembers Nick. 'The little female, we named Eeny, the more aggressive Meany, the smallest Miny and the most relaxed – a real smoocher – Mo. We accommodated them in a little den on a heat pad inside a wooden box.'

'Feeding sessions turned into amazing feasts – milk spilling in the most unlikely places. It was a riot! Four pups rolling, fighting and leaping in the milk dish.'

'Temperaments gelled with noisy wrestling and playing which evolved in fits and starts. Like all young marsupials, they craved physical attention and would climb up Kate and myself, hanging on by tooth and claw. One of their favourite tricks was to drag each other by the ears but despite the most persistent yanking and twisting, no harm seemed to occur.'

'Their newly erupted teeth were even, wickedly sharp at close range, giving a fair imitation of a miniature Great White Shark!'

When the four rascals reached 250g., they started to show interest in meat, accompanied by the beginnings of the devil's famous posturing, screaming and growling. They were soon climbing from their box, sliding along the lid on their bellies, paws pressed hard against the wall.

'Much to our amusement, like all youngsters, bouts of boisterous play would be suddenly interrupted by a sudden outbreak of sleep with no regard to occasion. Miny seemed a particularly enthusiastic climber, Eeny and Meany were forever wailing and tumbling while Mo much preferred to eat and sleep! Mo rapidly outstripped the others in size – eating up to 40% of his weight at one sitting!'

'All four devils incessantly sniffed, growled at, chewed and dragged whatever was available. Large bunches of car keys seemed particularly attractive and Kate and I surrendered our evenings to fits of laughter as bunches of keys rocketed around the floor, bravely propelled by four, eight, twelve or sixteen tiny, perfect black paws. On other occasions, they behaved like wild adults, with their ceaseless ghostly patrols, suddenly freezing to access some new opportunity, eyes and nose shining against their blackness.'

Meany – five- months- old.

At the peak of this packratting stage, a nerve-wracking incident occurred. Nick was away in Africa and Kate was leaving the team loose in the bedroom where she could keep her eye on them. Being nocturnal, the devils slept during the day and awoke muttering and seething before emerging as a gang to rampage about. That particular evening, Kate arrived home to find the house had been burgled.

'All cupboards were opened by the villains, searching for valuables,' continues Nick. 'Kate found all her drawers open with all her underwear gone. Worried at the thought of some "sicko", she remembered the devils and lifted up the mattress to see if they had been harmed. She needn't have worried. It seems after the break-in, they had come out and found all this "prey" exposed for them. So they cached it. There were the devils in a huge lingerie nest – Eeny with her head in some nickers, Meany loudly declaring his ownership of stockings, Miny peering from a bra cup and Mo thoughtfully chewing on a sock!'

'Once the devils no longer needed heated accommodation, our loudly complaining gang was banished outside – where they could have contact with wild devils through the slats, to gain their social graces.'

Eeny, Meany and Kate.

18

*Kate and The Gang
catching a spot
of sun.*

© NM

'They were transferred to a bush pen on the farm of Geoff "Joking" King, the most curious man in the world.   Here, they had a solid fenced area with secure den and a pile of logs from which they could see over the wall and familiarise themselves with their new home.   Rope laced across the top protected them from a surprise attack from eagles.   Peeping over the wall at Geoff's sons Angus and Hue, sent the devils into frantic retreat and they became nocturnal. The time for the final phase of "half-way housing" began.   With a huge fuss, I extracted them from their den, their ears were tattooed and ramps provided so they could come and go from the pen.'

'Eeny and Meany, consistent with their aggressive natures, chose to go while Miny and Mo stayed for a few days before taking their chances. Careful checks of devils roadkilled over the next few months, showed OUR GANG HAD MADE IT! With something like the chance they may have had originally– the *whole* idea of rehabilitation.'

'Eeny, Meany, Miny and Mo had been an education.'

'Talk about rewarding and educating!   Devils were *always* my favourite mammal and this fantastic experience has made that bias stick.   Not only that, but these little refugees were wonderful ambassadors, defeating the prejudices of more than one farmer.'

19

A rare moment's peace!
Swag was a special favourite of Kate's brother Josh.

PONIES OF THE MOOR

THE EXMOOR PONY SOCIETY offers The Exmoor Pony another chance, back from the brink of extinction.

In harsh, wild conditions, swept by icy winds, the Exmoor Pony can be found roaming through thousands of acres of moorland. From the pony's ancestors in Alaska, only the strongest survived and throughout the generations a sturdy, strong, stocky pony has evolved, capable of living unaided on the moor, finding his own food and shelter throughout the year.

The ponies are equipped with features to help them survive the long, harsh winters – long, oily coats provide protection from the rain and short, woolly undercoats provide the insulation they need.

But, The Rare Breed's Survival Trust has the Exmoor pony on it's endangered list. There are currently only 1,100 – probably twice as many wildcats in Scotland and as many Giant Pandas in China.

Dr. Sue Baker, from The Exmoor Pony Society, explains why the work of conserving the Exmoor pony *must* continue :

'It is impossible to say how long there have been Exmoor ponies roaming Exmoor. They are certainly mentioned in the Domesday Book but it is probable that they were part of the British fauna thousands of years before people came to the British Isles.'

'However, for many centuries, their fate was in the hands of whoever managed the Royal Forest of Exmoor for the Crown and after 1818, the landowners and local farming families.'

'Their closest brush with extinction came at the time of the Second World War. Many moorland ponies were stolen; most of the Anchor herd traced as far away as Carlisle. Presumably, their fate was to be food for hungry people in the wartime cities. Many Exmoor men went away to fight, so normal hill farming life was disrupted. Troop manoeuvres over Exmoor led to many of the Commons becoming unsuitable for stock grazing, gates were left open and animals strayed. By the end of the war, most

The Exmoor Pony – capable of living in wild, harsh conditions.

of the Exmoor ponies were taken back onto farms for their own safety. The effect of rustling and casualties had been to reduce the population down to just fifty animals. Only four were stallions.'

'This was a near catastrophic population crash which could so easily have heralded the end of the Exmoor pony.'

'But a remarkable woman, named Mary Etherington, was so horrified at the desperate state of the pony population, she set about rallying the Exmoor farmers to start breeding the ponies again. She lobbied the county councils to put in cattle grids to restore the boundaries of the Commons and she set about drawing attention to the breed's plight.'

'Slowly, the process of recovery was underway. The herds were re-established and despite the potential problems of such a small gene pool, by the early 1980's numbers had increased to about 500, by 1990 just under 800 and today estimates are around 1,100. Of these, only about 200 actually inhabit the moorlands of Exmoor.'

© Sue Baker

Wild and free -
mares & foal on Winsford Hill, Exmoor.

© HJW

Alone on the Moor.

Grazing on the Moor.

Mary Etherington had done a wonderful job of snatching the animal back from the brink of extinction but The Exmoor Pony Society knows only too well that the Exmoor's situation remains highly insecure. The Society exists to encourage and promote the breeding of the pure-bred Exmoor and also runs the Exmoor Pony Stud Book, which records the breeding of all registered ponies. They also publicise the ponies at many equine and agricultural events throughout the year.

'The Exmoor ponies,' says The Exmoor Pony Society, 'certainly warrant such efforts and need careful conservation. They are a very special type of pony, not altered by cross-breeding. The free-living herds are managed on a principle of minimum interference.'

'In Spring, the first foals arrive. They play from an early age, staying close to their mothers.'

'In Summer, the herd spends less time eating – their diet being nutritious grasses – and much of the day resting. The foals grow rapidly throughout the summer and become less dependent on their mothers. As tourists start to appear on the moor, the ponies generally favour quiet areas away from disturbance. Unlike many moorland ponies elsewhere, Exmoors rarely approach people.'

'By Autumn, as the amount of available grass declines, the ponies will vary their diet and grow their winter coats to ensure they are fully insulated and waterproofed. In late October, the foals are old enough to be weaned and they are gathered onto the farms for just one or two days to check for registration. The foals which are then released back to their moorland home, form the herds of a stallion with a harem of mares.'

'When Winter arrives, the food supply declines and life for the free-living Exmoors becomes extremely hard. Nature has endowed them with adaptations to aid survival in such harsh conditions. Their double-layered winter coats keep Exmoors warm and dry and poor fibrous food is digested to create internal "central heating". With less grass available, the ponies increase the amount of rushes and heather in their diet and eat large quantities of gorse.'

The Exmoor Pony can be tamed and trained
to become a steady, family pony.

'The Exmoor breed,' continues Sue, 'was *almost* lost forever. It's recovery, to the present day situation, is a positive example of what can be achieved. Yet with such a small breeding population even today, there is no room for complacency.'

'The work of The Exmoor Pony Society, and all those who work to conserve the ponies and their habitat, *must* go on.'

'Despite the ability to live independently, these remarkable, highly intelligent ponies can be tamed and trained. An Exmoor is strong enough to carry many adults, which can make it a true family pony. But for the last few years, demand for Exmoor foals has waned. Many breeders have chosen not to breed until the market revives. This may be prudent but what greater feeling of defeat can there be for those trying to build up the numbers of an endangered animal?'

'The Exmoor pony may have escaped extinction in the 1940's but has a *long* way to go before it is truly secure.'

The Old Man of the Forest – The Orangutan,
deep in the forests of Sumatra.

SOMALIA
THE BABY ORANGUTAN

THE ORANGUTAN FOUNDATION shows why the
Orangutan desperately needs our help.

Indonesian people call the Orangutan : 'Orang Hutan' – 'Orang' meaning Person and 'Hutan' meaning Forest. The orangutan literally is the 'Person of the Forest'.

Large, gentle, red apes from Asia, they are a highly intelligent species. They have the ability to reason and to think. Rarely setting foot on the ground, they live high in the trees, gracefully swinging through the forests, making nests of leaves and branches in the highest treetops. Everything they need, food and water, is found amongst the treetops and when the rain floods down, orangutans will be found sheltering under the largest leaves which act as umbrellas!

At one time, thousands of years ago, orangutans could be found throughout much of Southeast Asia. Now, they roam only on the islands of Borneo and Sumatra. Their continued existence is severely threatened by human greed, which may have HALVED the orangutan's population in the last ten years.

Without trees, the orangutan cannot survive. Yet the rainforest is being cut down for timber, much of which is converted to plywood. Millions of hectares of forest are also being cleared and burned to provide land for plantations, for crops such as oil palm. Fire is used, illegally, to clear the forest quickly and cheaply every year but in 1997/8 there was a drought in Southeast Asia and these fires burned out of control, destroying an area of forest the size of Belgium. As more forest is cleared, the orangutans have less space to live and less food. Sometimes, if they are very hungry, orangutans will come out of the edge of the forest to try to find food on the plantations. The people working on the plantations frequently shoot these adult orangutans because they are raiding the crops. If an adult female orangutan and her infant are found on a plantation, the mother is often shot and the baby orangutan is taken, to be kept as a pet.

Gaile Parkin, a volunteer with The Orangutan Foundation describes one such baby orangutan's miraculous survival :

'The baby orangutan that arrived at the rehabilitation centre in Borneo had been confiscated from his human owners who had been keeping him illegally as a pet. He was in an appalling state. Desperately malnourished and dehydrated, riddled with skin disease and barely able to open his encrusted eyes, he seemed hopelessly close to death. His similarity to the emaciated human refugees, then in the news, meant only one name for him came to mind : "Somalia".'

'At Camp Leakey he was to be given specialist care from Dr. Birute Galdikas but none of the staff had before seen an orangutan in such a shockingly poor state of health. No-one expected him to survive. The damage to Somalia was more than physical : the emotional damage had begun before his neglect at the hands of his owners. To be taken as a pet, he had in all likelihood been clinging to his mother as she was brutally killed.'

'At the camp, Somalia clung ferociously to Swedish carer Martina Bertilsson, refusing to let go of her for over a month and lashing out at anyone else who tried to take him. He was given one-to-one loving care but after a month he had put on only one kilogram of weight.'

'Gradually, miraculously, Somalia began to regain his strength and to feel more confident and secure.'

After nine months in care, Somalia began to venture away from his human carers and to bond with a fluffy orangutan toy.

*Increasingly independent, Somalia has fun
with a splash of water.*

'Eventually, Somalia was confident enough to begin integrating with the other orphaned orangutans at the camp.'

'One year later, Somalia was exploring the forest treetops and practising his developing skill of constructing nests from branches. He had developed a strong, feisty personality and although he was fairly independent by this stage, he was still being coaxed down from the trees to shelter inside at night for his own safety.'

'Today, Somalia is a healthy bundle of life. He has become the dominant orangutan among the group of juveniles released with him into an area of forest near the camp. His progress is still checked frequently when the rangers take milk and bananas out at feeding times.'

'When orangutans reach the age of eight, they decide to go it alone, whether their break is from an orangutan mother or from human carers. It is this natural desire for solitude that makes orangutan rehabilitation possible as it ensures their eventual move away from dependence on humans.'

'One day soon, Somalia will make the break and return fully to the wild. We hope his forest home will still be there to support him and his offspring, well into the future.'

'Somalia is just one of many orangutan victims. It was human ignorance and neglect that brought him to the brink of death; it is only human wisdom and generosity that can return his entire species from the brink of extinction.'

At rescue centres in Southeast Asia, staff are working to care for hundreds of rescued orangutans before they can be released into protected areas of rain forest. Scientists believe that less than twenty-five thousand orangutans remain in their natural habitat and that they may become extinct in the wild by 2020. Orangutans need to be free. They *need* the rain forest to survive.

~

A young Orangutan
swinging through the forests of Sumatra.

Bunnies, Bunnies, Bunnies -
Pass continually through the doors of
The Rabbit Charity.

Jack – The Second-Hand Bunny!

JACK - THE SECOND-HAND BUNNY
SPOK & AYOSHA - TWO BUNNIES IN LOVE

Beautiful, yet unwanted Bunnies,
THE RABBIT CHARITY is there to help.

The telephone continues to ring at The Rabbit Charity in London. Carolina James vividly remembers a call she took on one particular day :
'"Do you have a large male, lop-eared bunny at your Sanctuary?" the lady on the telephone asked. *"We recently lost our rabbit Barney and we would like one like him."* Barney had a big face and chocolate brown ears, he loved to play ball and followed her everywhere.'

'We don't encourage people to look for the same qualities in a new rabbit that their old rabbit had, to avoid disappointment. But as it happened, we did have a foster bunny, with brown ears and an exceptionally large face, that made him look like a soft toy, who also liked to play football and to rush up to anyone to be petted.'

'I described Jack's habits and main hobby (mating) and the lady was surprised at how much the two bunnies had in common. She was able to offer Jack the run of the house and a safe pen in the garden when she was at home. She also had an elderly dog who got on well with rabbits.'

'Because she lived so far from London, I sent her a photo of Jack and I was delighted when, a few days later, she made an appointment to come and see him. Jack lived up to her expectations – gorgeous, affectionate, following her like a puppy. I explained to her, being two-years-old Jack would be far less destructive than a baby bunny and as rabbits live on average seven to ten years, and as long as fourteen in some cases, Jack was still a young rabbit with all his life ahead of him.'

'The lady nodded but there was something on her mind.'

'Eventually, she said : *"I really would like a baby rabbit that hasn't been anyone else's pet."* '

Jack's downfall was the fact he was second-hand. Carolina looked at Jack – who a few weeks earlier had been taken to a veterinary surgery and never collected. With his big, sweet face and with so much love to give, he was just waiting to belong to someone.

But Jack's luck was soon to change. He scampered off to a new home with Helena, The Rabbit Charity's own treasurer, who was only too happy to adopt her special second-hand friend.

• • • •

Pebbles and Lollipop, Thumper and Clementine, Eddie Angora, Sweetpea and Willow – bunnies and more bunnies have continued to pass through the doors of The Rabbit Charity.

Then there was Spok and best friend Ayosha – another particularly happy rescue for Carolina and her charity.

'Spok and Ayosha arrived at our Sanctuary on the same evening and immediately fell in love with each other! Spok is a six-year-old brown and white French Lop who looks like a big slipper, especially when he takes a nap – which is often! Ayosha is the sweetest two-year-old Dwarf Lop with fluffy grey fur. Both have always had full run of the house and lived as part of the family.'

'Spok's carers had to part from him because they were emigrating to Brazil but Ayosha's owners did not want her anymore because she chewed the wallpaper.'

'They were both very loving and affectionate and always rushed up to me to be cuddled. After about five months, we were able to send two very contented bunnies off together to a new home with a large open-plan basement with a garden and a rescued guinea pig, which the bunnies adore!'

Jack & his new mate Campion.

Spok & Ayosha – Two Bunnies in love!

Cloud / Charlie.

Cloud, a beautiful grey and white rabbit, with big grey eyes, was heard digging frantically to escape from a cardboard box placed in a skip.

Once at The Rabbit Charity, it was discovered that "Cloud", thought to be a female bunny, was infact a male bunny who promptly had a name change to "Charlie"!

After three months of care at the Sanctuary, he went off to a new home to become best friends with a Netherland Dwarf bunny.

Says Carolina : 'Our Charity was set up to help rabbits and their carers. Although rabbits are the most popular pets after dogs, they have traditionally been considered children's pets and kept in a hutch at the bottom of the garden. The lack of a national charity devoted exclusively to their welfare was a sad reflection of rabbits' low status compared to other companion animals, so our plans to set up a bunny charity soon took shape.'

'We aim to rescue, educate, promote kindness and prevent cruelty to rabbits and because we are run by volunteers, every penny raised is used to help needy rabbits.'

'Visitors to our foster homes see our rescued bunnies living indoors! After being neutered, they are introduced to other rabbits and learn to live in a group. During the day they play in the garden in enclosures furnished with ramps, wooden tunnels, branches, footballs and toys. Our fosterers socialise the bunnies and work on behavioural problems before placing them in loving, permanent homes. Our charity has a non-destruction policy and values each bunny as an individual.'

'Our aim for the future is to buy a large sanctuary/education centre, which will include a rabbit veterinary clinic and a rabbit school, where people can learn about companion rabbits.'

Carolina wants people to realise that despite the fact everyone is looking for a baby bunny, adult bunnies need homes too.

Grey and white bunny Benjamin had been a child's pet and was often left without food and water. The children quickly grew tired of him. He then spent five years living on a garage rooftop without any grass or company.

When he was six-years-old, he arrived at The Rabbit Charity and his life turned around. He spends sunny days in Carolina's garden nibbling on the grass and digging up flowerbeds; evenings are spent curled on the sofa! A sweet and loving bunny, Carolina can now see the total contentment in his eyes.

'Our new Campaign,' she says, 'is "Benjamin's Campaign" – to encourage people to adopt adult and elderly bunnies; always overlooked by adopters yet they have *so* much to offer. Adult rabbits may have several years left and definitely deserve a second chance.'

Benjamin –
Leader of the campaign
to adopt elderly bunnies.

Benjamin –
taking a break
for some lunch!

HORSES, MULES &
THE DONKEY WITH TROUSERS!

*BROOKE HOSPITAL FOR ANIMALS offers help to
the hard working animals of Egypt, Jordan & Pakistan.*

Brooke Hospital for Animals has a mission :   'We aim to improve the condition and wellbeing of equine animals overseas by providing free veterinary treatment for the working horses, donkeys and mules of poor people in Egypt, Jordan, Pakistan and India and by advising and educating their owners.'

Very much a family charity, based in London, their work began way back in the 1930's.

When the First World War came to an end the British Government tragically sold off twenty thousand cavalry horses to buyers in Egypt. Horses that had survived the horrors of War were soon subjected to a life of toil and deprivation.

A great horse lover, Mrs. Dorothy Brooke, arrived in Cairo in October 1930. Shocked and appalled at the condition of these surviving horses, which she witnessed working in the streets, she at once set about putting an end to their suffering. She wrote a powerful letter to the 'Morning Post':

"In Egypt, there are still many hundreds of old Army horses sold at the cessation of the War.   They are all over twenty years of age and to say the majority of them have fallen on hard times expresses it mildly.   Egypt is not suitable to our horses : the heat, dust, want of water and the fact that European horses are bigger framed and require more food than the poorer class of owner is able to supply, all adds to their suffering.   The majority of them drag out wretched days of toil in the ownership of masters too poor to feed them – too inured to hardship themselves to appreciate the sufferings of their animals."

"Many of these old horses were born and bred in the green fields of England – how many years since they have seen a field, heard a running stream of water or a kind word in English? Many are blind – all are skeletons."

41

This letter advised the public just what was happening and to Dorothy's surprise the response raised today's equivalent of £20,000. She followed this up with more letters and within three years, with the assistance of her husband Major General Brooke and a small committee, she had bought the remaining 5,000 cavalry horses still working in Egypt. The impoverished owners were adequately compensated but most of the horses were over twenty-years-old and in the final stages of collapse. They had to be destroyed but they were able to end their days peacefully amid the care and attention to which they were all once so accustomed. Some, however, were cured and a small number were sent back to Britain to the paddocks of Dorothy's friends.

Dorothy Brooke had completed her task. But by rescuing the old war horses, she found she now had stabling facilities available for a greater challenge. And this challenge was soon to present itself.

It is difficult for westerners to appreciate the working conditions and hardships most working animals in developing countries have to endure. Their owners are, for the most part, very poor and so have the greatest difficulty in feeding and maintaining their usually large families.

Their horses or donkeys are their only means of livelihood and when these become old, lame or involved in an accident, most owners simply cannot afford either to release them for treatment or to replace them.

The result is that many of these animals literally die in harness. Impoverished owners manage with half a breadwinner; the animal's suffering - working for years with crippling injuries or diseases, long hours of work in temperatures of well over 100°f, little opportunity of water or a rest in the shade - cannot even be imagined.

So, in 1934 Dorothy Brooke, deeply moved by their plight, set up a free veterinary clinic – 'The Old War Horse Memorial Hospital' – The name has now been changed to : 'The Brooke Hospital for Animals'.

Dorothy stated : *"Our hospital stands to the memory of the twenty-two thousand of our army horses who served in the Middle East in the first Great War, to those who were killed in battle and to those, far less fortunate, who died in bitter servitude in Egypt, and to those found and ransomed who ended their days in peace and comfort in the stables that have now been converted into the Hospital that stands to their memory."* At last there was a hospital where owners, unable to afford treatment, could bring their beleaguered charges.

Today, the Brooke Hospital enables even the poorest and most hard pressed owners to maintain their animals in a caring manner.

Their animals are treated completely free and no animal is discharged before it is fit to work. If it is appropriate, the poorest owner, left without his mule and means of livelihood, will be given a small allowance. His animal will be treated, re-shod and badly fitted harnesses are mended. He will be requested to part with old, hopelessly lame, injured and worn out animals and will be given a contribution towards the cost of another. Everything is done to treat the animal but if it becomes necessary for an animal to be put down, if it is in no pain, then the Brooke Hospital let it have a few peaceful days – possibly the only proper rest it will have had in years.

After Dorothy Brooke's death, her work and aims to help millions of animals and their owners have been carried on down through her family with her grandchildren still very much involved in the hospital's expansion. At headquarters in London, volunteers work continuously to organise forthcoming events, fund raise, operate the Junior Club, all in the knowledge that all voluntary income is used directly overseas helping to support and treat more than 500,000 donkeys, mules and horses every year. In this way, up to two million people who are dependent on these animals, will survive.

The Brooke Hospital vets create a ripple of good animal husbandry, to reduce suffering, not just to treat it, with the ultimate aim : 'To run ourselves out of business!'

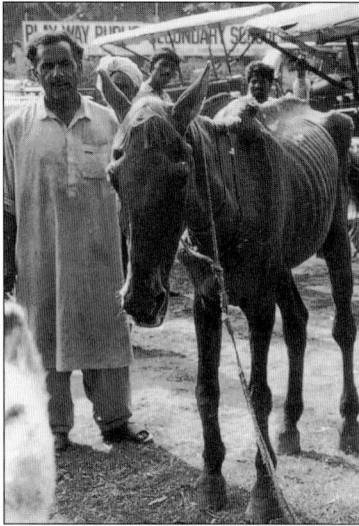

An owner, with his very poor horse in Gujranwala – Everything that Brooke Hospital is trying to avoid.

A typical Family in Lahore – totally dependent upon a very poor horse.

Photos © Brooke Hospital

An appallingly overloaded and unbalanced cart.
Brooke Hospital vets advise owners on all aspects of animal
management.

A Brick Kiln
Worker with his
dreadfully
emaciated horse.

Enlightened
ownership and
freely available
support will be
crucial to the
well-being of this
man, his mare
and the family
they both have to
support.

Much of the Brooke Hospital's most valuable work abroad in India, Jordan, Pakistan and Egypt is done in the city and country markets and at the animal's work place, using mobile teams.

The Mobile Clinics visit these areas several times a week and evidence of their success in the areas where they have worked can be seen in the greatly improved condition of the working horses and donkeys.

'Our vets educate large numbers of owners in basic animal welfare and in the importance of early treatment of diseases. Gradually the owners realise it is in their own interest to care for their animals and to seek out our help.'

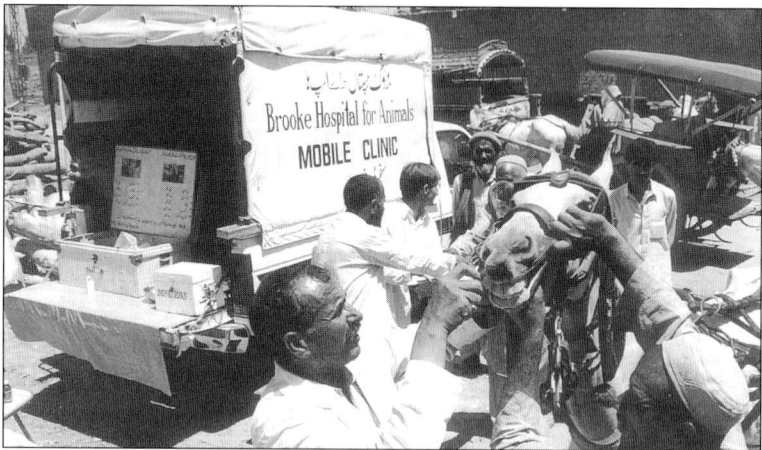

The Brooke Mobile Clinic Team.
Hard at work in Peshawar,
the vets will see as many as one hundred animals a day.

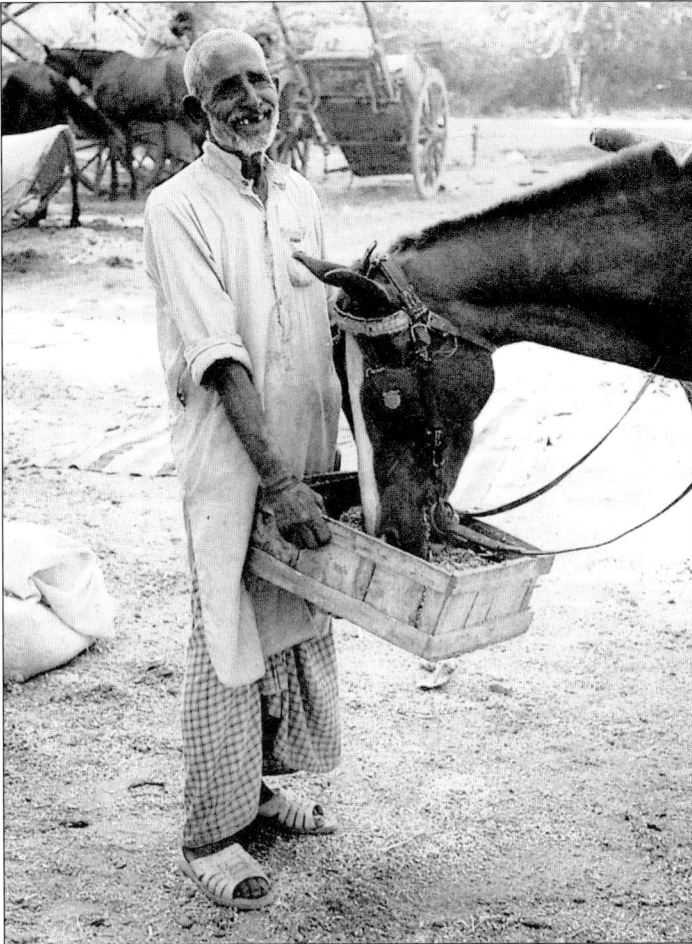

*A consultation with the Brooke Mobile Clinic
leads to a happy owner and a happy horse.*

In 1988 Princess Alia, King Hussein's daughter, requested that Brooke Hospital establish a clinic at Petra to help the 350 horses that carry tourists to the entrance of the ancient city. While the horses wait for their passengers, they are now able to use the specially built shelters and troughs. After a hard day they could well have travelled 15kms in very hot, dusty conditions.

The Hospital has made three key contributions to the lives of the horses at Petra : good farriery, shelter and water.

A Farrier at work.

Good Shelter for the horses of Petra.

A Brooke water trough at Petra –
a lifeline for horses working in the heat.

In Pakistan, despite the advent of the car, the day of the working animal is by no means over and up to four million horses, donkeys and mules are at work every single day.

In 1991 Brooke Hospital set up their first mobile veterinary team in Peshawar in the North-West Frontier province of Pakistan. With the use of an inpatient clinic, six teams now work in and around the city providing over 7,000 treatments a month.

Two years later, a similar mobile team was set up in Lahore. This now provides 10,000 treatments a month. The mobile teams go to wherever there is a concentration of animals such as vegetable markets, railway stations and road junctions.

Brooke Hospital's Director of Veterinary Services speaks of a typical day in Pakistan :

'The walls of the Old City of Lahore lie just behind me. The road in front is a nightmare of traffic. A torrent of modern machinery tears through the more slow-moving horse-drawn tongas. Heat, dust, stench and fumes grip at your throat; the colour and sound of true poverty assault your eyes and ears; tempers flare and fade in the rush hour traffic. Yet, in the distance, a Brooke Hospital mobile team attends to a line of patiently waiting horses.'

'A huge variety of conditions is seen on the streets in Pakistan –a horrendous gaping saddle wound, originally caused by a dirty, ill-fitting saddle; a longstanding lameness in both hind legs, joints worn out by hard work; a debilitated animal whose bones show through the skin, badly fed; a high fever .... Onwards, ever onwards the team move down the line.'

'Travelling north through Pakistan, South-East of the town of Peshawar lies Surezai – an area with a concentration of brick kilns. Poor, overladen donkeys carry the bricks to and fro. However, in the heart of the kilns, the Brooke Hospital has it's own field clinic – a simple quadrangle with three sheltered walls under which the animals can quietly stand, eat food and drink water. Here they find peace and contentment. Severely injured animals can be transported back to the main clinic by ambulance trailer. These clinics amaze the local people but pleasure is beginning to replace initial suspicion at the help we can give.'

At work in the Brick Kilns.

Most problems that Brooke Hospital vets come across are the result of poverty and ignorance. The owners are so desperately poor and often have to make a choice between food for their family or food for their mule. But many injuries and diseases that the vets treat are preventable. Poor harness, inappropriate feed and poor shoeing are all major causes of injury.

So the vets carefully work with owners and improvements are made. As soon as they become knowledgeable and conscientious, the poorest carters can feel proud to have a beautifully kept horse or donkey.

51

In Egypt, the Brooke Hospital has six centres – in Cairo, Alexandria, Luxor, Aswan, Edfu and Mersah Matruh - all with qualified vets, veterinary assistants, farriers and supporting staff who carry out thousands of treatments each year. Since it opened in 1934, the main hospital in Cairo has never turned an animal away. They have an operating theatre, dispensary and medicine store, farrier's shop, small animal clinic, fly proof stabling and two large paddocks for convalescents. They are supported by an ambulance and two mobile clinics.

A Foal born at the Brooke Hospital in Cairo.

The mobile clinics visit seven country markets around Cairo each week and three Zabbalin camps. These camps are inhabited by a coptic Christian community, the poorest of Cairo's poor, who earn their living by collecting rubbish from the city in donkey carts. The people sift through and sell or use anything that can be salvaged. They rely totally on their animals. The animals would go untreated if the owners had to pay.

Zabbalin Donkeys at work on the outskirts of Cairo.

Many owners in Egypt courageously manage under permanent conditions of crisis. A poor woman with her donkey, in a Zabbalin rubbish collecting community, still manages to feed her donkey well.

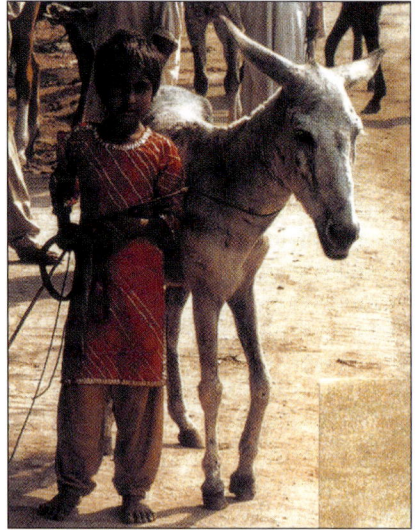

A Little Girl & her donkey.

Brooke Hospital came across the pair on the streets of Lahore. The donkey was almost as small as the girl. He had injured his shoulder and could hardly walk. This was a crisis for them both. If the donkey were not treated, rested and allowed to recover, he would be crippled for the rest of his life and condemned to work in pain. Worse still, he could suffer ritualistic branding at the hands of a local farrier. This would not only be totally ineffective but also excruciatingly painful, as these operations are never performed under anaesthetic.

An owner holding a roadside drip, provided by Brooke Hospital's Mobile Clinic.

The Mules in the Bhatti mines, south of Delhi,
work a 12-hour day.

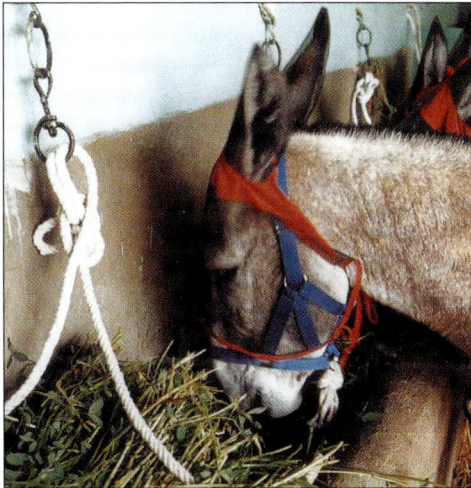

A donkey enjoying her time in the clinic at Luxor.
Recently, a mule on discharge from the clinic escaped from her cart,
crossed the city and returned to the stall where she had spent three
contented weeks for 'a little more of what she fancied'!

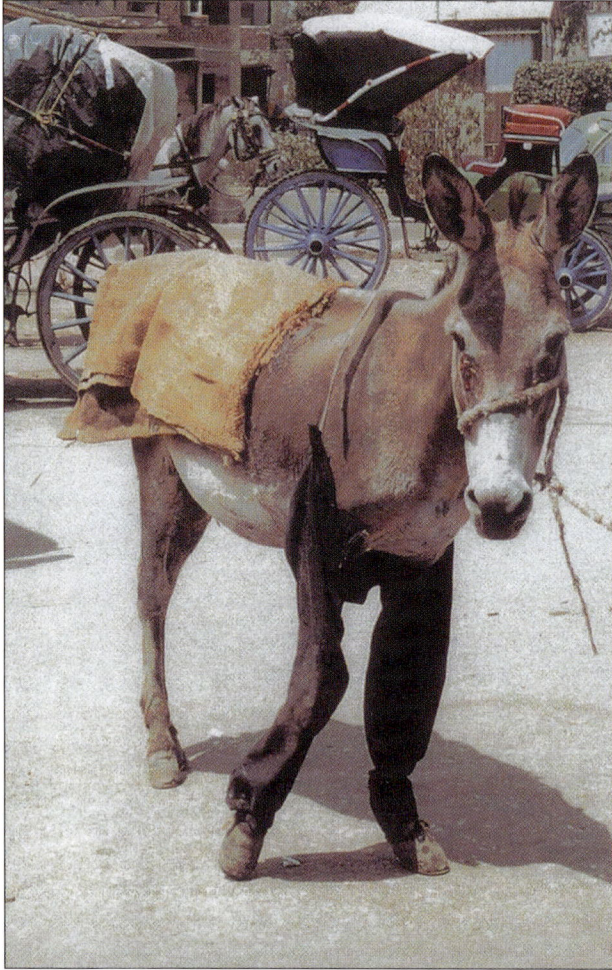

The Donkey with Trousers!

Mark Lainchbury remembers a comic moment amongst the hard work faced by the Brooke Staff, on his recent visit to Shirbin, a town in the Egyptian Nile Delta :

'The streets are quiet before dawn breaks and a team of Brooke Hospital staff set up the mobile clinic they have brought from Cairo. Colourful awnings are tied to provide shade and large quantities of veterinary supplies are neatly laid out. Very soon the inevitable line of donkeys and horses begins to form. Many are used extensively by townspeople for transporting themselves and their products.'

'First Dr. Salah rasps sharp teeth in a horse to the left. Dr. Emad examines a horse with a severe cough across the road. Dr. Reda advises a family on the care needed to resolve a saddle sore. Dr. Mustapha cleans a wound. The team is busy. The sun rises and with it the heat, the noise and the flies. The local people are friendly. "When are you coming to stay?" they ask.'

'"Homar be bantalon gaa" – the word goes round the town square – "The Donkey with Trousers is back" ! Work grinds to a standstill as everybody stops to look. This donkey became quite a favourite. The poor animal had an unpleasant dermatitis that itched furiously. He had bitten his front legs in a hopeless attempt to reduce the irritation. The owner used a splendid pair of trousers to cover the front legs, hanging them from the animal's neck with a set of braces! It's a simple and sensible attempt to reduce the self-mutilation but did not deal with the cause of the problem. He was a comic but sad figure standing dolefully in the queue of horses awaiting treatment. Fortunately the work of the previous days had made him better, the irritation subsided rapidly and the appropriate drugs cured the problem.'

'It was another successful day and no-one would forget the donkey that arrived in such a fine pair of trousers!'

~

THE CANADIAN BEAVERS

BEAVER WATER WORLD & REPTILE RESCUE
work daily with the continual abandonment of wild animals.

A visit to Beaver Water World will place you in the company of a variety of rescued reptiles and some truly delightful creatures – a large, happy family of Canadian Beavers.

'Our Canadian Beavers arrived in 1995,' says Stella Quayle, who runs the reptile rescue in Kent. 'Beavers are such gentle creatures, so intelligent and so family orientated. All the family look after the babies and they are very secretive and protective of their young.'

'Our first beaver baby, Twiglet, was born a year after their arrival and I will never forget I cried with emotion the day his mother brought her litter out to see us. The baby just sat in the palm of my hand and it was a very emotional moment. The following year, we had another litter of five.'

'They can all be seen every day in our beaver pool, swimming with the rest of their family. The best time to see them is in the afternoon as having been busy all night gnawing at bark, they are not early risers!'

'So far we have re-homed three beavers to a wildlife centre in Scotland, two have gone to Herne Bay in Kent and several have been adopted by local Beaver Scout groups. There are still people willing to build waterways and lodges on their land so the protection of this delightful animal is continuing.'

One of the Beavers comes out of the pool to say 'hello!'

Busy Beaver repairing it's dam.

Lunchtime with Stella and her Beavers.

Safe at last at Reptile Rescue.

For Stella, her work with rescued reptiles all started in 1980 with Rivet, a small Indian Python. One rescued snake led to another and in due course Big Boy, the alligator, came to join the collection.

Now, a well-planted clay pond has become home to a naturalised colony of red-eared terrapins; the aviaries contain parakeets and exotic birds; there are ornamental fish ponds, rabbits and chipmunks, pythons and boa constrictors, king snakes, corn snakes, iguanas, skinks, lizards, bearded dragons and water dragons.

'Over the years,' she says, 'many reptiles have been abandoned on our doorstep. On a typical Saturday morning we might find several basilisks (lizards from Central America) or iguanas, left in the middle of our drive, in a pillow case. They could have been left for several hours on a chilly night. It can be quite an interesting and tense situation trying to decide what animal is in the pillow case as it moves around the tarmac – rather reminiscent of three boy scouts fighting in a tent!'

'I ask myself so many times, why it is people abandon these animals? What is the matter with people to make them do this? Many owners just do not realise what they are taking on when they obtain a reptile as a pet. However, we will care for them all. Somehow we manage to find room for them and for some we will find new homes. We try very hard to create near natural conditions in peaceful and secure settings.'

'We do our best to discourage the public from purchasing wild caught animals and are currently promoting conservation projects such as the Rain Forest Project in Belize, which is protecting areas of iguana habitat.'

'I would so like to see the whole issue of reptiles reviewed at government level. Because reptiles are sold in pet shops, they are considered by the public to be domestic pets. They are most definitely *not*! They are wild animals, taken from the wild and the fact that they choose to tolerate us is something people should be eternally grateful for. However, they are wild, independent creatures and should *never* be brought over from their country of origin.'

ARK – Animal Refuge Kansai,
high in the mountain forests of Japan.

ANIMALS
OF THE EARTHQUAKE

Victims of the Kobe Earthquake find shelter at ARK –
the only Sanctuary in Japan with open doors.

However remote the area, in whichever country of the world, an English woman can often be found running an animal sanctuary.

High on what was once just a bare mountainside, off the beaten track in a quiet region of Japan, you will come across Elizabeth Oliver and her trusty volunteers. At ARK – Animal Refuge Kansai – dedicated animal lovers are working to improve the plight of homeless, abandoned and ill-treated animals in Japan. Although this country has many genuine animal lovers, animal welfare lags way behind other developed countries.

There are very few organisations and virtually no shelters for homeless animals in Japan. Animals found on the streets and handed in to the Authorities (hokensho) are held three days before being killed by inhumane methods. Tagged animals are not returned to their owners – they are killed.

Some Japanese regard pets as status symbols; as disposable objects. When the fashion changes, out goes the 'old' pet and in with the 'new' one. Many dogs are kept tied on short chains. When they bark incessantly from boredom, they are cast aside. Japanese companies move employees around at short notice; so the family pet is given up. All over Japan unwanted puppies are dumped in their thousands. Many die terrible deaths through starvation, traffic accidents or are killed mercilessly by the hokensho. Those that survive and breed become feral, which people condemn as wild and dangerous. Japanese, although western in outward appearance, are very Asian in thinking.

ARK therefore has a monumental task on it's hands. It has to adapt to the Japanese situation and Japanese way of thinking. Currently two hundred dogs, one hundred and sixty cats, goats, a pig and a silver fox all find refuge here. Many came to ARK as a result of the Great Hanshin Earthquake of 1995.

For Elizabeth, it was the end of life as an English teacher in Japan, helping animals in her free time. It was the beginning of a new life, as full-time guardian of a family of animals at ARK.

Elizabeth recalls : 'One second in time changed my life forever.'

'Never did I think, as I was jolted out of bed in the early hours of January 17th 1995, that an earthquake would change my life so much.'

'I had been told earthquakes come in a series. Maybe the first one wasn't the main one. The aftershocks rumbled on. If that was a small one what would the real one be like? I lay in bed trembling.'

'But first light revealed the peace of the morning – a beautiful sunny day – but all communication with the outside world was cut off. I started walking my dogs but not a soul was in sight. I began to have a growing fear that the rest of the world had gone and I was the only one left alive.'

'Eventually the voluntary staff at ARK started to trickle in with stories of the horrendous mess in their houses, the blocked streets, fallen buildings, virtually impassable huge cracks that had appeared in the roads. ARK's larder and freezer had food supply for a month but I was more concerned about having enough food for the animals. So later in the day I ventured out to a shopping centre in search of supplies. Like a war scenario, the place was jammed packed with shoppers but all the shelves were empty – everyone was panic buying, hoarding for the worst.'

'As the days passed and the scale of the tragedy unfolded, it became clear what a huge task lay ahead. Priority was on rescue but then what? We had at ARK facilities for perhaps a hundred dogs and fifty cats but how would we cope with the potentially thousands of animals made homeless in the quake? In other countries, with established animal welfare systems, there is a built in evacuation mechanism to rescue and save animals in cases of natural disaster. In Japan there are no facilities for holding animals except the hokensho, which are geared only for killing.'

'The International Organisations were quick off the mark offering us immediate help but this in general was refused by the Japanese government. Finally a Swiss rescue dog team was allowed in.'

'But within a week, help arrived from the IFAW from the USA. A huge, jolly woman of Dutch origin, who spoke a dozen languages, became our supreme organiser. Annamieke quickly transformed my kitchen into her headquarters, demanding extra telephone lines and demanding we went shopping. "If people don't eat properly, they can't work," she said, so we went shopping! She cleaned the supermarket of food and spent a fortune!'

'Annamieke was at ARK for nearly a month. She seldom left her 'desk' and was up most nights sending faxes, emails and writing reports. She had a wealth of 'useful' people she could tap for information, materials and money. She used to call me M3 – micro management maniac – because I always had the tendency to try to do everything myself.'

'Our most pressing need became facilities for the animals, who by now were coming in from the earthquake areas thick and fast. We just didn't have the space at the main ARK site so we rented a field. Having land was one thing but we needed to erect some kind of temporary building. Suddenly building materials were like gold, impossible to get even at a price. So we opted for vinyl houses, the sort used for agriculture.'

'People who already knew about us had started bringing their animals in. John, a dog we had re-homed from ARK came in completely traumatised. He had been buried under his owner's house when it collapsed. It took him several days to stop shaking. On the same day, Baxter arrived. His owners, now homeless, were refused hotel accommodation because they had a pet. One man and his family managed to secure a hotel room but their thirteen-year-old blind, maltese dog was refused entry. So the family members took it in turns to sleep rough on the streets with their dog.'

'Many owners, homeless and not knowing what to do about their pets, were in desperation asking vets for euthanasia. It was urgent therefore that we reach these people. We prepared hundreds of notices : "ARK's emergency facilities for earthquake animals". Then came the problem of distributing the notices.'

'Unlikely help came in the form of a gang of Hell's Angels from Tokyo, who thundered up on roaring bikes to offer their services as volunteers! Night after night they rode around the earthquake areas distributing notices, pinning them on telegraph poles, broken houses, wherever they could. People started to respond and soon we were deluged with requests to take in animals.'

'A small group of us then set off to Kobe, one of the worst affected areas, to see the situation first hand. We carried rucksacks filled with pet food and water and carry cages for cats. On route for Kobe, the scene in whichever direction we looked was one of devastation. Street after street, just piles of memories of where houses had been. Some were tilted at grotesque angles threatening to topple at any minute. Multi-storey buildings looked alright at first glance until you realised some of the storeys were missing. We walked in the direction of the Nishinomiya City office, which was under siege. People waited in line with buckets for water or rice balls. The sounds of sirens were deafening. What we hoped to achieve was a drop in the ocean but we *had* to start somewhere.'

'Earthquake animals were tethered along the roads, others in cages inside tents. A man in a wheelchair had been quickest off the mark in organising the animal rescues and within days he was sheltering hundreds of animals. But his act of kindness and genuine wish to help animals was to turn sour. He was innocent of the big, bad world and he knew nothing about the gangster-dominated underworld of dog breeding in Japan. Big guys in the form of the Japan Kennel Club and a well-known pet food company soon muscled in and took over his operation. They knew that the prosperous residences in the Hanshin basin would provide a rich harvest for valuable pedigree animals. The pedigree dogs were whisked away to 'new homes' in Tokyo while the man was left with the mongrels. Distraught owners, appearing daily in search of their pets, found they had all gone.'

'Several months later, the man appeared at ARK asking if we could take the old, sick mongrels he had been left with. His act of kindness had been sadly exploited.'

'We saw cats hiding in the rubble, some feral but many obviously house cats. Cats had tended to stay inside the wreckage of their former homes for shelter and security. The noise of sirens and general chaos all around terrified them. We were faced with a heart-breaking choice – which cats to rescue? We managed to catch one grey tabby and we left a name card on the collapsed gate in case the owner wanted to claim her. We continued walking around for eight hours.'

'On our return to ARK, Annamieke was determined to visit Kobe herself. But not by walking! "A helicopter is the answer!" she said. Those of us from small countries tend to think of helicopters being used by the army, air ambulance or the very rich – certainly not as a means of transport for the ordinary person. But Annamieke was from America where it is a normal way to get to inaccessible places quickly.'

'The journey to Kobe took only twenty minutes. Acrid smoke still rose from the fire blackened voids where communities had once been. Roads were like sand dunes in a desert. The force of the quake had virtually turned the whole island upside down, where the helicopter had landed, forcing sand from the bottom up through the asphalt onto the surface. It was a sight I shall remember until my dying day. In the heart of Kobe people sat on pavements outside shattered homes. We found Elle, an old dog with bad skin, whose neighbours said had belonged to a couple who had burnt to death. We put Elle on a lead and took her along with us.'

'The area we steeled ourselves to visit was a district where burst gas mains had erupted into fires that raged unchecked until nothing and no-one remained – just skeletons. It looked as if a massive bomb had struck. It was enveloped in a black silence. We now had two cats and Elle the dog. We saw several frightened dogs but they evaded our efforts to catch them.'

'In the following weeks animals continued to come into ARK thick and fast. Owners managed to bring their pets in, often in tears at having to part with them. Our van would set out late at night to pick up animals, arriving back early in the morning. None of us had any proper sleep for several months as we picked up and cared for animal after animal.'

'It is hard to imagine the trauma these animals had been through; all their day-to-day normality had gone. Many suffered depression, others fear. Stress related symptoms lead to illness. I came to realise just how few dogs are socialised in Japan. It is a point of pride with owners to show their dog is loyal to them and only to them, which meant we had to deal with many fear-biters. Slowly, with love and patience we succeeded in turning many of these dogs around. When owners came to visit later on, they were amazed by the transformation. "Is this really my dog?" they asked.'

'Every animal came in with it's own story. Some stayed only a short time, some returned home after a year, others are still with us today. Some owners could not take their dogs back as they were unable to cope, affected by the trauma of the earthquake. One dog Riki, a fourteen-year-old, pined endlessly for his owner and died slowly of a broken heart. Fourteen-year-old Goro was luckier. His owners visited once a week until their house was rebuilt and he could go home. That *was* a happy day! Takatori, blind and deaf, was rescued from Kobe and ended up with a wonderful new home.'

'Popeye, an endearing mongrel with one eye missing, was found weak and shivering in the rubble of a building. Another night, eleven maltese terriers arrived from a breeder whose house had collapsed. A dear little dog we named Kobe, as a symbol of all the animal victims of the quake, gave birth on the night she arrived.'

'Then there were the rabbits! A telephone call came in asking if we could temporarily take in about sixty rabbits. We made the owners promise to neuter the males and prepared the enclosures. A small yellow car came up the track to ARK with smoke pouring out, clearly about to catch fire. The doors opened and we realised to our horror all the rabbits were loose in the car!'

Poor Riki pined endlessly for his owner.

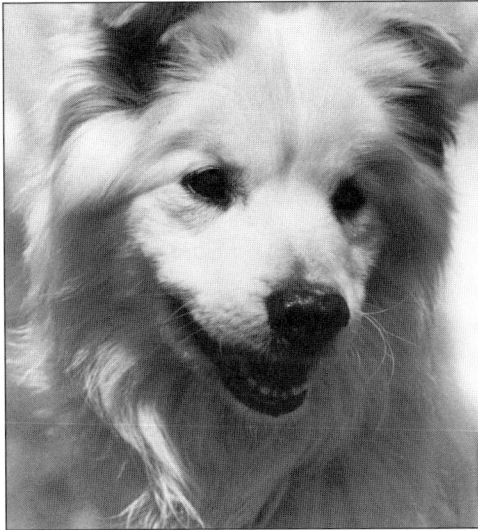

Takatori – blind and deaf,
yet still found a wonderful new home.

Two of ARK's cheerful volunteers
walking the earthquake victims.

'It was like a scene from "The Keystone Cops", everyone running around with cages, trying to catch bunnies! World War III was about to start in the bunny world as boss buck rabbits started to terrorise the rest. We sub-divided the groups of bunnies over and over again. We found a new home for two but the owners would not hear of it. They were furious and we had to get the two bunnies back. To us all the rabbits were identically grey but this family knew each one by name. The owners never expressed any gratitude for the time we spent caring for these rabbits and we were all relieved in the end when they came in yet another clapped-out car to collect them.'

'Thanks to a lot of media attention, the stories of the earthquake animals reached people's hearts. Normally at ARK it is very difficult to find homes for adult animals – everyone wants brand-new, cute puppies and kittens. But after the quake it was different. Suddenly "earthquake animals" became desirable and everyone wanted one. It didn't matter if they were old or handicapped, people wanted in some way to help animals in distress. So many animals we never imagined in our wildest dreams would find a new home, did so. Many of the animals already at ARK found good homes too.'

'Several volunteers from abroad ended up taking earthquake animals home with them. Two volunteers, from the UK, took home two cats who found wonderful new homes. Annamieke too couldn't resist adding to her mountain of luggage to carry an earthquake puppy home. On arriving at Detroit she demanded VIP class for both herself and her dog's flight home to Boston!'

'Many owners came to ARK holding photos of pets that had disappeared. One elderly woman, whose beloved fifteen-year-old dog Asuda, going blind and deaf with old age and who had been sleeping beside her, had run out of the house and through a huge hole that had opened up in the garden wall. She had been searching for weeks, never giving up hope. It had taken her nearly a day to come up to ARK in the hope he might be safe with us. Sadly, we had to tell her he was not.'

'On a happier note, other dogs, even a year later, were re-united with owners who thought their pets had been lost forever.'

'Many earthquake cats are still at ARK. Tama, was nearly crushed to death when her house collapsed. The experience left her so traumatised that she refused to come out of her box for two whole years when people were around. At ARK she was still very nervous but became much better. As each day passed she learnt to trust people again and lived to the grand age of eighteen with my eight other cats in my house.'

'Mikan, a massive ginger and white cat was rescued and boarded at ARK, yet her owners never came back to take her home again. But she is now sleek and healthy, ARK has become her permanent home and her firm belief is that everybody who enters her pen, should give her a cuddle!'

Mikan.

Tama.

'Altogether ARK took in nearly five hundred animals. What would have happened to these animals if we hadn't been there? ARK never received a single yen from the huge fund for earthquake animal victims which had accumulated from private donations around the country. We were told the funds were being held for "the next disaster".'

'The earthquake was a watershed for ARK. We could never go back to being the small intimate group of volunteers we had been. We lost friends who preferred the old ARK. But we gained a lot of volunteers and people still remember "the forgotten earthquake animals at ARK".'

Walking the dogs around ARK.

'Sometimes I think the tunnel is very dark and it's impossible to find a way out of it but I have decided to light a candle rather than complain of the darkness.'

'Some days, when I get telephone calls from irresponsible people who want to get rid of their pet or from those who have rescued an animal but are unable to keep it, I feel depressed at the enormity of the problem. We can't accept all these animals but if we refuse, what will people do with them? Throw them away? Take them to the hokensho? The options in Japan are nearly nil.'

'But other times, to see a terrified and physically scarred animal brought in, to watch it's progress as it heals, as it slowly gains confidence and begins to trust humans again, this is a reward in itself.'

'If you love animals, they love you in return. It's as simple as that.'

~

Elizabeth – A friend to all the earthquake animals.

Cheeky Chappie –
Bush Baby George.

GEORGE BUSH – THE BUSH BABY
ANGELS DELIGHT – THE GOAT
& CORNFLAKES – THE COCKEREL

LORD WHISKY SANCTUARY's ever increasing animal family.

Deep in the Kent countryside, Margaret Todd can be found each and every day, dedicating her time to a multitude of animal friends at The Lord Whisky Sanctuary.

'After over thirty years in animal rescue,' she says, 'starting with my first dog at thirteen years old, the excitement of a new animal coming in never ceases to fail me. It is in the eyes that look at you, searching your face for re-assurance, sometimes frightened, sometimes holding back, sometimes appealing and sometimes completely disinterested, the more-or-less given up look.'

'It was this last look that I received from the biggest pair of eyes ever seen in a little face!'

'It was on a very cold winter's night, when everything was frozen. I answered the door to a man who had rung earlier in the evening with "something in a box that he had found at the top of a tall tree in a pigeon's nest"!'

'I carefully opened the box expecting to see some sort of bird but instead there was this little creature, a little bit like E.T., with these enormous eyes and little ears. A tiny Bush Baby had come to join our family of animals. He felt so cold and lifeless that the first thing was to provide him with some heat and get some warm fluid into him. This he took in a sort of "couldn't care less" attitude, which continued for several days.'

'Then one evening, this lovely little hand with perfect fingers appeared and took some food from the dish. His body started to feel warmer and from then onwards he started to come alive. We found out his likes and dislikes, goat's milk being one of his favourites - bringing about a good recovery, meal worms, cheese and lots of fruit, the occasional rusk or digestive biscuit and scrambled eggs.'

Native bred, this bush baby's parents were probably imported from America about ten years ago when they were very popular and sold at pet shops. Because they are nocturnal and impossible to house train, bush babies do not make very good pets, so the craze soon ended. This little one was one of a pair who had escaped from an aviary. His friend was never found and almost certainly perished but this was the lucky one, arriving at the sanctuary when he did.

They chose to name him George Bush – after the American President and bush baby George now enjoys a wonderful life, spying on the world and all his animal friends from his tree hideaway. Totally spoilt, he likes a cuddly dressing gown to cuddle up on. If it is taken away to be washed and replaced with towels and blankets, bush baby George will go into a sulk!

'George is very precious to us,' adds Margaret. 'Although nocturnal, he loves a daytime cuddle and will soon forget the time of day if you have something special for that lovely little hand to take. He will stay with us for the rest of his life and, who knows, perhaps one day a Georgina may be found to keep him company!'

• • • •

A tiny baby Goat, born at the Lord Whisky Sanctuary to Tizzy, an elderly Nanny, also became a very special friend to Margaret and her family. Unfortunately, Tizzy was unable to feed her and she was too weak to suckle another Nanny.

'She was very small and underweight,' remembers Margaret. 'We wondered if she would survive but with encouragement to take the bottle, she gradually pulled through.'

'We named her Angels Delight – so determined to pull through, always happy and as she got stronger with her lovely personality and sense of fun, she became a true 'delight' to everyone and everything that got to know her. Born in March, she represented everything that spring is about – as beautiful as a buttercup and fresh as the daisies in the field. In fact, just simple pleasures – "Angels Delights".'

Angels Delight.
'Represents everything that Spring is about.'

Cockerels on their own, or with several hens, make very interesting pets. Over the years, the Lord Whisky Sanctuary has had many, including three that were left in the forest.

'They are *so* colourful,' says Margaret, 'and what a lovely sound every morning – your own alarm clock welcoming the dawn. It is a sound greeting a new day, for which we should all be thankful. It comes completely free and causes no harm to anyone. I feel it *must* be better than all the man-made noises we have to put up with. I feel very sorry for people who don't welcome it.'

'Our Cornflakes is a cockerel that a young girl brought to the gate and begged us to take. He had lost his home due to the noise of his dawn chorus. Unfortunately you can only have one cockerel with a group of hens and we had our quota, but having seen Cornflakes, we had to take him. He slept in the stable yard and soon settled in.'

'Cornflakes lived quite happily as a bachelor. Then one day, the hens came through from the paddock and he literally took one under his wing before the rest were put away. Cornflakes and his bride Puff Wheat were inseparable but after a while, he started to sleep on his own.'

'Then, one lovely sunny morning, there he was with Puff Wheat and their family - hatched under the wood pile. What a proud family they are!'

'Cornflakes is always very well behaved, strutting in the spring sunshine and he loves a cuddle!'

'His loud "COCK-A-DOODLE-DOO!" in the morning is a sound I always enjoy, like the smell of new hay when I walk in the barn and the wonder of all the beautiful creatures that are in our fields, each one a different character, each one special to us in their own way.'

Cornflakes, the Cockerel –
A most handsome bird.

'Cock-a-doodle-doo! Just look at my family!'

Photos © LWSF

SASHA & COLUMBINE

THE SHETLAND PONY & POT BELLIED PIG
& ALL THE GANG AT ANIMAL TRACKS!

International Animal Rescue offering help around the World.

Jo and John Hicks have been at the forefront of animal welfare since the mid 70's campaigning against fur shops, vivisection laboratories, circuses, deer hunting, but it had always been their dream to establish a charity that would help animals world-wide.

A few years ago, John's long-standing friend Miss Tillyer, kindly gave John the funds to make that dream come true. Miss Tillyer had always been a devoted animal lover, rescuing animals throughout her life and with her continued kindness and generosity, International Animal Rescue has become a tremendous success.

Together, John and Miss Tillyer purchased Animal Tracks – an old working farm in need of gutting and major improvements. Today, Animal Tracks is an education.

The sanctuary nestles in sixty acres of some of Devon's most beautiful countryside and over one hundred rescued animals, from marmosets to shire horses and lambs, ducks to squirrels, pot bellied pigs to geese, can all be found, content and happy. Specialised accommodation has now been provided for animals of all types, all housed in real comfort. Large deer paddocks, large fox pens and a brand new pond for the ducks have been created.

'The animals at Animal Tracks now all have stories with truly happy endings' says Alex, IAR's Manager.

'Basil, our Badger at Animal Tracks, was so ill when he was found, he stood very little chance of surviving. He was only about ten-days-old, his mother had been killed and he had crawled out of the set in a desperate search for food.'

'For three weeks we dripped fluids down his throat, day and night and because of the intensive care needed to pull him through, he cannot go back into the wild as he would be unable to

Baby Basil.

A happy life now at Animal Tracks.

Hazel makes herself at home.

Pansy.

Larch, Felicity and Chloe.

fend for himself.   But he is a very happy badger and we are happy to have him living with us.'

'Hazel, our squirrel, fell out of a nest during a storm when only a few hours old.   She now protects John's house as her own territory and will not allow any strangers indoors!   She is mad about mashed potatoes and chocolate and becomes furious when she is only permitted small quantities simply as a treat!'

'Most of our sheep come from people who have reared them from lambs for the freezer and then find out that sheep have personalities and characters.   We are then asked to salve their consciences by taking in the animal they can no longer face killing.'

'Pansy was the only survivor of a farmer's neglect – he allowed his ewes and lambs to starve to death while he was on holiday.   She was only a few hours old when we took her in and has grown up with us.'

'IAR have an ever-expanding family of goats.   Larch, a very impressive goat arrived at Animal Tracks with three other goats from a small sanctuary without the right facilities.   Felicity and Chloe, our two Angora goats, were simply unwanted.   Now all enjoy more freedom and country air than they could ever have hoped for.'

Almond and SingSong live a contented life
with Damson, Easter, Crumpet and Carbon the Aberdeen Angus.

*Rainbow & Byron
& Dennis.*

© IAR

'We have many Parrots in our care at Animal Tracks.'

Calypso.

'Calypso is one of a growing number of parrots. Despite their attractive appearance, they do not make suitable pets as they require constant attention and are very destructive. The trade in parrots has almost caused the extinction of many wild breeds and has been responsible for unimaginable cruelty. The majority of parrots die from sheer terror or from their cramped and appalling travelling conditions.'

'Regrettably, wild birds are still being trapped and we appeal to everyone to boycott pet shops which sell birds that have been caught in the wild.'

'Rainbow, the Parrot and Byron, the Cockatoo were both rescued from a pet shop in Worthing. Now, they happily live together with our other rescued birds.'

'Dennis, an African Grey, was rescued after spending fifteen years locked up in a cage, little larger than a standard budgie cage. He was in a greenhouse with no heat during the winter and suffocating heat during the summer. When rescued, he did not do or say anything. He simply sat hunched on his perch all day, every day, year in, year out.'

'The sooner caged birds are made illegal, the happier we will be. Dennis is now in an aviary and finally can be heard whistling and cheerfully calling out all day long!'

'At Animal Tracks, horses and donkeys graze in the fields. Chala is the horse we saved from slaughter and like most of our donkeys, Rosemary was an outgrown, unwanted child's pet. We were asked to take her in when the children lost interest in her. Several months after this, she surprised everyone by producing 'Violet', who is now bigger than her mum!'

Chala,
Rosemary & Violet.

© IAR

'Sasha, the Shetland Pony was sent to a hunt kennels to be slaughtered to feed the hounds. Luckily, someone hearing of her plight rescued her and brought her to us.'

'Although she is elderly and was in poor condition when she arrived, she was soon restored to the peak of health and has spent many happy retirement years with us. She became close friends with Bella - another of our horses who we also saved from being destroyed.'

International Animal Rescue
Devon.

'Our Sasha'.

Smart, heated homes for the Vietnamese Pot-Bellied Pigs.

Two pot-bellied pigs were the pets of two children who kept beating them with sticks. When rescued, not surprisingly, they were terrified of all humans but now realise staff at IAR mean no harm.

Clover.

Columbine wallowing in Mud glorious Mud!

A group of Ducks enjoy their new pond.
In the background, the smart new duck houses.

Myrtle -
A resident rescued
Goose.

The Gang!
These Ducklings were rescued after their mother had been killed. They have grown
up to live a life of utter contentment, strolling around the sanctuary or swimming in
the pond, waiting for their dinner to be served to them!

Dawn, with a poorly dog in Goa.

*Dawn & Sonia visit some of their rescued dogs
at Calangute Market in Goa.*

A considerable call on IAR's limited funds, is the vital work they do abroad. They have successfully taken on projects other charities would consider too difficult.

With millions of animals roaming the streets of India, the level of suffering endured by these poor creatures is some of the worst in the world. However, the Indian people are not a cruel race and despite the devastating poverty, the compassion shown to animals would put many developed countries to shame. But poverty being such a deep-rooted problem, the authorities simply do not have the resources to treat injured animals on the streets. So bodies of cats and dogs are an everyday sight on busy Indian streets.

Because the suffering is so extensive, IAR have established a permanent clinic in Goa – thanks mainly to Dawn Hurst and Sonia Hillage.

Desperate for a two-week holiday break, Dawn and Sonia took themselves off to Goa. But all thoughts of a rest soon evaporated almost as soon as they were off the aeroplane.

'Our holiday was to be short-lived,' says Dawn. 'We were immediately aware of the massive population of dogs and cats that lived and survived on the streets with no owners, living amongst the chaotic traffic and hectic surroundings of India's fastest growing tourist region. Many were suffering terribly with maggot infested wounds.'

'On our first day we found a tiny, pathetic looking young dog suffering from almost every skin disease imaginable. Desperately wanting to help, we faced an uphill struggle to find help from anywhere. We knew *something* had to be done about the suffering of animals in Goa so we sent an urgent fax to IAR.'

John Hicks took a flight immediately to Goa to see how he could help. A vet arrived from England and over the following months, hundreds of animals were neutered, vaccinated and treated for injuries.

Once a large property had been purchased, plans were made for a first class surgery to be built and in terms of stopping animal suffering, the project has been a tremendous success.

A sick and dying kitten on the pavements of Goa.

Help arrives and lucky kittens rest after a filling breakfast at the new IAR Centre in Goa.

IAR's efforts in Malta have also met with great success, to the extent that the Parliamentary Secretary for the Environment publicly stated that IAR had "been the catalyst for change in Malta". Their work in Malta covers every aspect of animal welfare.

They have been running a vigorous campaign to protect millions of migratory birds which are being shot and trapped every year. Non-stop fundraising enabled them to purchase a high-powered boat. This is now on permanent loan to the Maltese Police to stamp out illegal bird shooting at sea.

© IAR

IAR's high powered boat to stop illegal shooting of migrating birds at sea.

'We have established the only Wildlife hospital in Malta,' says Alex, 'and we have a specialised marine section to tackle the problems of stranded dolphins, the illegal trapping of turtles, we monitor marine pollution and organise beach clean-up operations. Our boat can be used when there are oiled seabirds that need catching and they can be treated at our bird hospital rather than being left to die.'

'Stray cats and dogs are another major problem in Malta, so we have been running an on-going neutering campaign.'

'Our greatest success was the discovery of a so-called dog "sanctuary" – the Manoel Island dog sanctuary – where as many as fifty dogs and puppies a week were dying from neglect. Hundreds of dogs were literally lying on top of each other. They were breeding and newly born pups were often just eaten by other dogs. Terrible dog fights were breaking out and dogs were left to slowly die from their injuries. The place was filthy and alive with rats and for food, scraps were left in the sun all day, covered in flies, before being fed to the dogs.'

'Within hours John Hicks had arranged for a vet to attend to the many sick animals. John spent three days working from dawn to dusk improving conditions for all these poor creatures. He then took a flight back to Britain, put a team of ten people together and was back in Malta in three weeks to build new facilities for the dogs.'

'Even after all this work, the person in charge of the animals still neglected them and conditions deteriorated again rapidly. As if that was not enough, after all the effort and money spent by IAR, the person in charge was now making conditions even worse by starting to take in cats! Needless to say, the cats were terrified with all the barking dogs.'

'So we had to take the problem to the highest level of government. This resulted in an armed police raid. IAR were then able to run the sanctuary on behalf of the government.'

'This was a huge commitment, which had not been planned for but because of the terrible suffering, we did not hesitate. Veterinary surgeons were called in and two IAR staff arrived from Britain and soon the place was gleaming clean and the dogs bouncing with health. A massive advertising campaign was started to find the remaining one hundred dogs good homes.'

'Thankfully now Manoel Island has been closed down and the circle of suffering has finally stopped. There is still a long way to go before the problems with stray and unwanted dogs and cats can be resolved in Malta but IAR's hard work and determination will go on.'

The filth covers the floor where the poor dogs lived. Without the stench and the flies, the photo fails to show just how bad it really was.

IAR's sparkling clean pens, separating dogs from bitches to stop the fighting.

One of the poor, sad little creatures.

Volunteer Heidi, with one of the many puppies saved from almost certain death.

Photos © IAR

'IAR's work and influence is spreading to countries world-wide. We are now looking at projects in countries as far away as Peru and The Seychelles.'

'At our main headquarters in Devon we only have four paid staff who, along with our executive Director, receive only a minimum wage. We believe money sent to us should not be spent on top executive salaries – money sent in for the animals, should be spent on the animals. And it is.'

RED ROO
THE KANGAROO

Australia's QUAMBY WILDLIFE SHELTER
offered their help to a Kangaroo, who now has
no intention of leaving!

Life, for Ivy Hawken and her fellow carers at Quamby Wildlife shelter in Bacchus Marsh, is very busy. Ivy has worked with the wildlife of Australia for over thirty years, caring for the injured and the orphaned, creatures that would otherwise be left to die. Most are victims of humanity; only about one-fifth are genuinely sick or injured by self-inflicted accidents such as a kangaroo misjudging the height of a fence or birds of prey crashing into high wires.

The day a certain kangaroo came into Ivy's life was the day a beautiful friendship began.

Red Roo - named because at the end of the season her old coat takes on a rusty red colour before shedding out into a new blue coat – found herself hit by a car on a road beside Quamby Wildlife Shelter. For several weeks Ivy found herself with a very sad Roo. Her injuries were relatively minor but she was fretting. They kept her in one of the smaller enclosures, which was well sheltered with plenty of grass but she would only eat bread offered by hand. She completely refused to eat grass.

'A month passed,' says Ivy, 'and Red Roo had got back on her feet but she was a very depressed and sad girl. We decided the best thing was to let her loose to do her own thing. By this time she had accepted us completely, as though she had known us all her life. She particularly liked my husband!'

'The day we opened the gate of her enclosure, there were quite a few roos grazing on the lawn. Red Roo came half way out, spotted the others, reared up on tip-toe and began shaking all over. For almost five minutes she studied these strange animals, then turned and went back into her enclosure. Nothing would coax her out! So we left her to settle down and work it out for herself.'

Red Roo - checking out her countryside.

Red Roo & Pal aboard the trailer.

'Eventually, after the roos had moved on, out came Red Roo to check out the immediate area very carefully. She saw my husband in the car port and with a huge skip, hopped stiffly up to him.'

'When kangaroos are pleased or happy for any reason, they move with a skipping hop. It is a kind of no-rhythm hop where every part of their body goes in different directions at the same time whilst the animal is in mid air. All kangaroos do this – but only when they are pleased. Red Roo was so happy to see my husband, when she got to him she put her paws on his arm and stood high to sniff his face. They had a great chat together! When my husband headed indoors, Red Roo was *not* going to be left behind!'

'She followed and tried very hard to get inside. She looked hurt and confused when she was firmly told *her* place was outside. It took weeks for her to accept this and she learned to content herself with standing at the window that gave her the best view inside. We have now had her for some four years and she still places her paws on the sill and gazes in!'

Raised as she was, Red Roo has implicit trust in man and that anyone would want to hurt her is, in her mind, completely inconceivable. Over a period of time, she has thoroughly explored her new world and made herself known to most of the regulars in the area. She has had many adventures due to her continual curiosity.

'One particular dry summer,' remembers Ivy, 'when green grass in the bush was non existent, all properties set in bushland followed the strategies for fire prevention. As our shelter had a reasonable supply of water, the surrounding areas were kept green and lush. As the summer wore on and the land around changed from green to gold as the grass seeds ripened, with no rain at all, even the tough native grasses lost what little appeal they had. The country took on a brown and sun-bleached tapestry, typical of Australian inland.'

'But the area around us took on the appearance of an oasis and every evening the roos would come down out of the bush to mow our grass.'

'Red Roo was *not* impressed with this alien invasion. She didn't like kangaroos and she preferred fresh, green grass ungrazed by others. So, while she was always around the house somewhere during the day, at night she sought better grazing in an area where the wild bush roos wouldn't go.'

'A neighbour, a kilometre away, had also kept the land surrounding his house green, thick, lush and very attractive to Red Roo on a hot summer night. Having no fear of the humans who lived there or their dogs, Red Roo innocently grazed, poking into the corners where the grass was freshest.'

'Being a full grown female, Red Roo on tip-toe stands as high as a man. So, when the lady of the house stepped outside her back door to breathe some cool fresh night air, with no torch, she was shocked to find herself in total darkness eye to eye with a six foot Roo on tip-toe! She did not know who Red Roo was or infact that she even existed at that time. She gave Red Roo as much of a start as she got herself! She backed off, naturally thinking this was a great male and extremely dangerous as such! She now looks back on the incident with quite a bit of amusement but she does like to stress however that it was not funny at the time!'

'Over the time we have had Red Roo, she has become firmly placed in our hearts. Obviously the people who raised her were kind, loving people who treated her as their equal. I don't know how she was in the situation to be hit by a car but I am sure it was not intentional. She has adopted us as her substitute family, totally and without conditions.'

Roos come down from the Bush to check out the lush green grasses.

Red Roo enjoys some breakfast.

'On another occasion, Red Roo fancied a day out at a sand quarry further down the valley. Off she hopped for a closer inspection.'

'Early in the day, the shelter got a telephone call from the quarry, enquiring if I could come and remove a roo from the premises. It seemed that when staff turned up for work, there was a large roo relaxing in the porchway of the office block! No-one felt inclined to go up the narrow stairway past the animal so they busied themselves doing other things while the telephone rang it's head off unanswered. Their hopes that the roo would move quickly enough when the machinery got moving were realised but not quite with the end results that they envisaged.'

'It was natural for everyone to assume that this was just a confused or sick wild animal; that a tame roo should be wandering around just never occurred to them. Nobody wanted to risk injury by physically confronting this unusual visitor. "Leave it to the experts" they thought!'

'So, when I got the call, the kangaroo had moved off the porch but promptly settled itself on the weigh-bridge. Attempts to shoo it off were met with a display of how tall it could get and how tight it could clasp it's arms to it's chest! This was very intimidating to the staff, who at this stage were pretty desperate, as no trucks could come in or go out without being weighed first. The entire quarry was by now brought to a total standstill by one roo. Our own Red Roo!'

'I went over there armed with a loaf of bread as I knew this behaviour was definitely not that of a wild, confused animal. Only Red Roo would do this – and I swear, when I arrived, she was smiling the whole time!'

~

Kangaroo & Joey
in the Australian countryside.

BEAST, HONEY & FRIENDS
THE PEOPLE'S PETS

All given a helping hand by the PDSA.

The PDSA is Britain's largest veterinary charity, caring for poorly pets since 1917, when Maria Dickin, the charity's founder, opened the first dispensary to alleviate the suffering of animals belonging to the poor.

With hospitals throughout the country, they now give a wide range of free veterinary treatment to around 1.4 million sick and injured pets each year. They receive no government funding for their veterinary services and rely entirely on public generosity through donations, legacies and fundraising. Their work is of great importance to animal welfare and they need the support of pet lovers everywhere. Since PDSA clients cannot afford private veterinary bills, if the charity was not around, many animals would not get the care they need.

Pets ranging from dogs and puppies, cats and kittens, budgies canaries, rats, mice, hamsters, rabbits and gerbils have all passed through the doors of the PDSA.

Staff at the PDSA are confronted with different problems each and every day and a visit from a handsome black cat from Dundee, called Beast, proved no exception.

Being a somewhat curious cat, Beast found out the hard way that exploring the human environment uncovers hidden household hazards!

Anne Cooper's much loved family pet couldn't resist the temptation to find out where all the water went to when it left the sink. And promptly, his foot got stuck down the plug hole! No amount of gentle cajoling could ease the paw out so the plug hole was unscrewed and Beast, his poorly paw and plug hole attached were all taken to the PDSA veterinary centre in Dundee for emergency treatment!

Senior Veterinary Officer Andy Cage was on duty that evening and remembers the little black cat.

'Beast was in a lot of pain and considerable distress,' says Andy. 'His paw was very swollen and the pad was split. A general anaesthetic was needed in order to remove the plug hole as, by this time, Beast was becoming increasingly anxious.'

After a night's rest at the veterinary centre, where staff monitored his progress, Beast was well enough to go home –albeit with a slight limp.

'Beast did not live up to his name at all,' says Andy. 'He was very brave considering how confusing it must be for a cat to have a plug hole stuck on his paw!'

Beast's owner adds : 'Without the prompt help of the PDSA, Beast might not be bouncing around on all four paws as he is today!'

• • • •

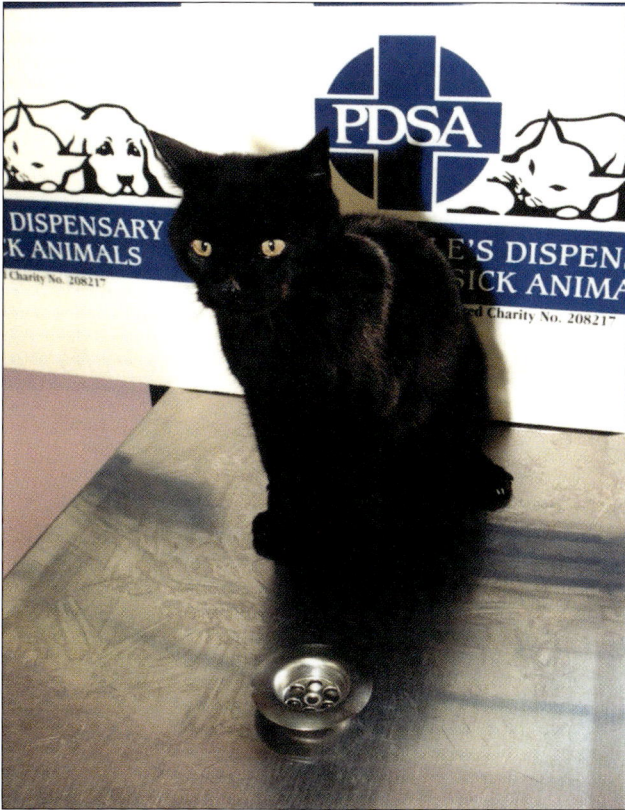

© PDSA

Beast - left drained after his encounter with a plug hole!

The theory that "cats always land on all four paws" was disproved when Finn, a playful kitten, fell from a window.

Despite the fractured pieces of bone in his leg, Finn enjoyed his stay at the PDSA in Edinburgh. However, his owner deserted him, despite repeated calls and letters from the charity.

But Finn was soon to find his very own good Samaritan – a PDSA volunteer – and now the lively and mischievous cat is bounding around getting into lots more trouble at his new home!

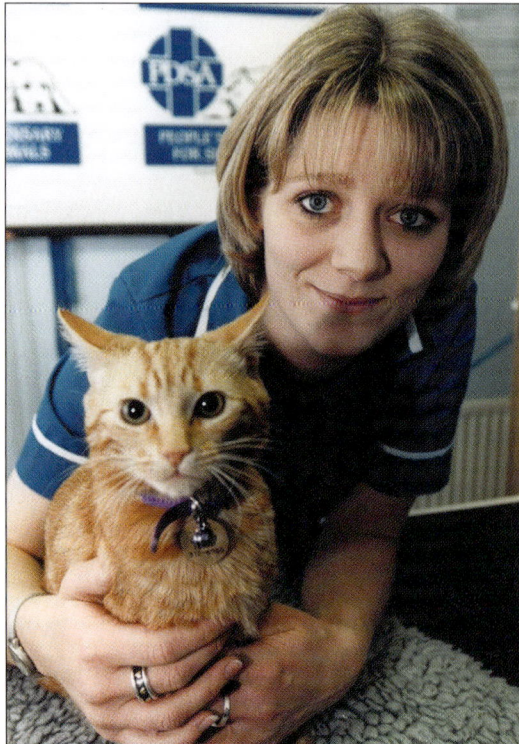

Finn - with PDSA Veterinary Nurse Lisa Parker.

Gizmo - with relieved owner Joanne Goudie.

When four-year-old Gizmo was hit by a car and unable to move, he faced a long road to recovery. Three fractured limbs meant he would be left with only one leg if they proved beyond repair.

But the Chatham PDSA hospital once again came to the rescue and Gizmo today is as good as new.

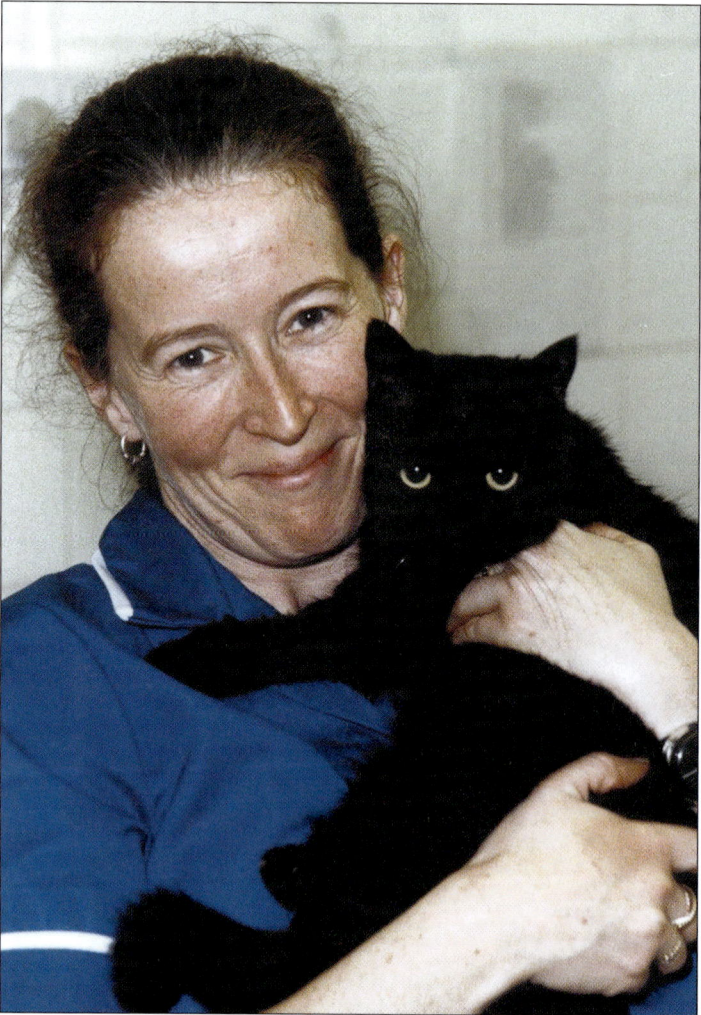

Honey - with PDSA Veterinary Nurse Lisa Williams.

When three-year-old Rebecca Rogers innocently decided to give her grandmother's cat a wash to assist with her daily grooming, she very nearly killed her with kindness.

Honey, the much loved four-year-old cat belonging to Mavis Rogers, was too placid to protest when she was shampooed down with a mixture of toilet cleaning gel and pine disinfectant!

As soon as Mavis realised what had happened, Honey was taken straight to the Liverpool PDSA for emergency treatment.

'Honey arrived at the centre salivating profusely, with her mouth open and having difficulty breathing,' remembered Senior Veterinary Officer, Chris Symonds. 'After being covered in caustic substances, the poor cat had tried to clean herself which resulted in severe burns to her mouth and throat. This meant she was unable to eat and drink.'

Honey, a model patient, stayed at the centre for four days, while staff constantly cleaned and groomed her as she was unable to do this for herself. She was put on intravenous fluids and given antibiotics and pain killing injections.

Gradually her ulcerated mouth and throat began to heal and staff encouraged her to eat a little tuna fish on her own.

Says Honey's owner: 'I don't know who was in more distress – me or the cat – when we first arrived at the PDSA! Thanks to the prompt treatment and care, Honey has made an amazing recovery.'

• • • •

It may be true to say that a little of what you like is good for you but cross-breed Jack, from Fife, recently found out that more than a little can very nearly be fatal!

Young Jack had managed to steal and eat 300gm. of chocolate – enough to kill a small dog.

Chocolate contains theobromine, a chemical which is harmless to humans but poisonous to dogs.

Luckily Jack was sick before he had absorbed enough of the chemical for it to be fatal.

Says his owner : 'We will certainly be sticking to a less indulgent diet from now on!'

• • • •

Poor Arthur from Drumchapel became the repeated target of cruel air gun attacks in his home town.

On the first occasion he arrived at the PDSA centre in Glasgow with a small wound at the back of his neck and left shoulder. Staff agreed Arthur had been lucky and surgery was not needed.

A year later, Arthur returned to the PDSA with difficulty in breathing and a small wound in his chest. This time two pellets were removed by surgery.

A month later, Arthur again got caught in the cross-fire and was hospitalised for two days. Once again Arthur had been lucky and the pellet had not caused any fatal damage.

To avoid another catastrophe, his owner says : 'Arthur will be my *indoor* cat from now on!'

~

Jack.

Arthur.

Oceania.

OCEANIA
THE SEA TURTLE

MEDASSET releases the Ambassador of the Oceans, and continues to campaign against the exploitation of Mediterranean Sea Turtles.

Like all sea turtle species around the world, the Hawksbill, so named for it's hawk like head, is on the endangered species list. With an incredibly beautiful hard, amber/brown shell, and head and flippers of gold with dark brown patches, it is widely considered the most beautiful of the turtle species.

In the past, the hawksbill has been intensively hunted to make turtle-shell jewellery and artefacts. Frequenting the tropical waters of coral reefs and with an appetite for sponges and other denizens of the reefs, the adults can grow to 90cm. and reach 60kg.

One such hawksbill turtle, a baby of just 6cm., arrived in Paris in 1993 having been smuggled into France by a traveller returning from some 'unknown islands'. The Society for the Protection of Animals came to her aid, passing her on to the Oceanographic Institute of Paris and then to the Aquarium of the Oceanographic Museum of Monaco.

Here 'Oceania' as she was named, proved she was a survivor. She thrived and further developed her liking for the high life on a gourmet diet of mussels, shrimp, squid and clams.

Five years later she had blossomed into the full beauty of her species 38cm. long and weighing 6.2kg.   But the Monaco Aquarium, already having one adult hawksbill on exhibit, were now anxious to find her a new home.

Without hesitation MEDASSET – The Mediterranean Association to Save the Sea Turtles – went into action!

Five months of faxes, emails, telephone calls and planning resulted in a 'hotel' booking for a short stay at an aquarium in Maderia and a passport to enable Oceania to once more take to the air. All this was to enable her to once again continue her travels back swimming in the warm waters of the ocean - her natural habitat.

The day MEDASSET had waited for arrived and articles and photographs appeared in the French language press around the world. Oceania, having spent the night in a tank with two conger eels and two grey triggerfish, was carefully wrapped in sea-water soaked towels and placed in a styrofoam box within two wooden crates. Placed aboard the aeroplane, she was allowed to travel in the passenger compartment. Calm and peaceful throughout the flight, on landing she began to show signs of excitement.

She was then transferred to a wooden sailing boat off Maderia, tagged and measured and as the sun sparkled on her beautiful gold markings and amber shell, Oceania was gently lowered into the sea. She was back in her Ocean!

As soon as she became accustomed to her surroundings in the water, she swam below the surface with regular calm strokes of her flippers in a straight line towards the North-West. Divers swam with her until they ran out of film, their lives brightened by the exotic beauty.

Adds MEDASSET : 'In Greek mythology "Oceania" was the eldest of the three thousand daughters of Oceanus and his wife Tethys, nymphs frequenting the seas and shores. She was renowned for her beauty and her good and compassionate heart.'

'We do not know what adventures await this modern 'Oceania' but she will, we are sure, be a fine Ambassador of the Oceans.'

Sea Turtle of the Mediterranean.

MEDASSET has been working since 1988 on the conservation and study of these most endangered of species. Their most recent campaign is to stop the slaughter and trade of sea turtles in Egypt.

Lily Venizelos explains : 'By visiting the Alexandria fish market in Egypt, you will be shocked to see the sea turtles lying on their backs………. The turtles are slaughtered in the early mornings of Friday and Sunday, when there are sufficient customers to share its meat and drink its blood - Egyptian women believe that this will increase their fertility. The turtles' shells will be dried with salt and sold to shops and the students of the Faculty of Fine Art. If there are not enough customers, the turtles will be left alive until the following Friday or Sunday. During that period they are lying on their backs, without food or water.'

'This appalling sight illustrates that Egypt still does not abide by the legislation concerning the protection of sea turtles.'

Over a five-month period MEDASSET made frequent visits to the fish market in Alexandria, to record the number of sea turtles on display. Both loggerhead and green turtles were seen, amounting to a total of one hundred and thirty five turtles, either sold directly to customers or to fish restaurants. They were brought to the fish markets by the fishermen as a result of trawling and bottom longline fishing. The fishermen claim to catch the sea turtles 'accidentally'.

'In recent years, there have been increasing efforts to bring the non-implementation of the legislation to the attention of the Egyptian government by environmental groups,' says Lily. 'It has to be ensured that the legislation in Egypt covers the protections of nesting areas, foraging and wintering grounds. At the moment, those exploiting the sea turtles are either not aware of the laws or are not willing to abide by them and give up a profitable trade. We *must* stop the slaughter.'

MEDASSET is providing a more active programme of environmental education and public awareness, targeting the locals, tourists and fishermen. Strong penalties need to be introduced to protect the turtles in Egyptian waters.

A further project for MEDASSET is beach pollution.
Lily Venizelos explains : 'The Mediterranean shores are shared between people and many marine organisms. Every year millions of marine animals die world-wide due to many types of pollution but it is the small pieces of personal garbage, casually discarded on the beach, which are the most damaging.'
'One of the most common and destructive substances is plastic. A transparent plastic bag in the water, looks very similar to a jellyfish, the favourite food of many sea turtles, resulting, once the bag has been ingested, in either the blockage of the digestive track or the suffocation of the turtle. The impact of 'small garbage' on the marine environment is immense.'

Rubbish from the beach,
collected at sea – found in
an Albatross' nest!

© Frans Lantig /
Centre Marine Conservation
Washington DC/ MEDASSET

'Above all else, think about the consequences of your waste - if you don't, there is an innocent victim waiting for a slow and painful death.'
'A little care on our part can mean life for a turtle. Without our help they will lose the battle!'

ACKNOWLEDGEMENTS

The Author would like to thank the following individuals and the Animal Sanctuaries listed below, for all their help in the compilation of Another Chance III.

ARK – ANIMAL REFUGE KANSAI
Osaka-fu, Toyono-gun,
Japan 563-0131

Elizabeth.Oliver

BEAVER WATER WORLD
Tatsfield, Nr. Westerham,
Kent TN16 2JT

Stella Quayle

BROOKE HOSPITAL FOR ANIMALS
London SW1Y 4DR

Richard Searight

INTERNATIONAL ANIMAL RESCUE
Ash Mill, South Molton
Devon EX36 4QW

Alex Pawley-Kean

LORD WHISKY SANCTUARY FUND
Stelling Minnis
Nr. Canterbury, Kent CT4 6AN

Margaret Todd MBE

MEDASSET
London W1Y 7DF

Lily Venizelos

PARKS & WILDLIFE SERVICE
Hobart, Tasmania 7001
Australia

Nick Mooney

PDSA
Priorslee, Telford
Shropshire TF2 9PQ

Hilary Nelson

QUAMBY WILDLIFE SHELTER
Bacchus Marsh,
Victoria 3340, Australia

Ivy Hawken

THE EXMOOR PONY SOCIETY
Glen Fern, Waddicombe,
Dulverton, Somerset TA22 9RY

Dr. Sue Baker

THE ORANGUTAN FOUNDATION
London NW1 4RP

Lisa Brooker
Lisa Mather

THE RABBIT CHARITY
PO Box 23698, London N8 OWS

Carolina James

Front Cover Photos : IAR, LWSF, Corel UK.
Back Cover Photos : ARK, IAR, BWW, LWSF, The Rabbit Charity,
Brooke Hospital, Corel UK.

THE DOGS & CATS WHO BRIGHTEN THE LIVES OF SOME OF BRITAIN'S MOST POPULAR PERSONALITIES :

Celebrity Pets
cats and dogs who befriend the famous

Claire McClennan

Ernie Wise, Ken Dodd, June Whitfield, Valerie Singleton, Barbara Cartland, Jenny Seagrove, Leslie Thomas, Robin Cousins, Rosemary Conley, Russell Grant, Anthea Turner, Terry Waite, Lorraine Kelly, Kriss Akabusi, Wendy Richard and many more.

'A nice gentle read about famous personalities and their pets.'
Editor, Pet Dogs

'The book is lovely.'
Eastenders Actress, Wendy Richard

''Tis a great wee gift for animal loving pals.'
Actress, Pat Coombs

'A lovely book.'
Radio/TV Presenter, Valerie Singleton

AUTHOR SIGNED COPIES AVAILABLE ON REQUEST

RRP £6.99   ISBN : 0-9526944-0-9

A COLLECTION OF
TRUE DOG STORIES -

UK and International –
From many leading Animal
Charities & Sanctuaries.
Abandoned, neglected, victims
of cruelty, rescued by animal lovers
and offered a new happy life.

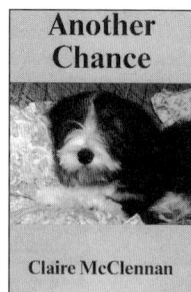

Another
Chance

Claire McClennan

A Lovely Gift Book
Many Photos - Detailed Artwork.

It's a Lovely Book.'
Living Free Animal Sanctuary

'Delightful! We are sure it will be very popular.'
NAWT

'We enjoyed the book very much.'
Friends of the Animals

'A collection of twenty four compelling
Dog Rescue stories which will help raise funds
and promote the work of Animal Welfare Shelters.'
Vesna Jones, Greek Animal Rescue

'Heartening tales of Dogs. *Another Chance* will appeal
to anyone who cares about animals.'
PDSA

AUTHOR SIGNED COPIES AVAILABLE ON REQUEST

RRP £6.99

ISBN : 0-9526944-1-7

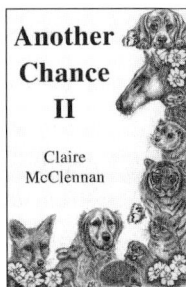